The Hidden Fortune within the Mind and Beyond

The Hidden Fortune within the Mind and Beyond

Barbara Brusky

BALBOA.
PRESS
A DIVISION OF HAY HOUSE

*Balboa Press books may be ordered through
booksellers or by contacting:*

*Balboa Press
A Division of Hay House
1663 Liberty Drive
Bloomington, IN 47403
www.balboapress.com
1-(877) 407-4847*

*Because of the dynamic nature of the Internet, any web
addresses or links contained in this book may have changed
since publication and may no longer be valid. The views
expressed in this work are solely those of the author and do
not necessarily reflect the views of the publisher, and the
publisher hereby disclaims any responsibility for them.*

*The author of this book does not dispense medical advice or
prescribe the use of any technique as a form of treatment for physical,
emotional, or medical problems without the advice of a physician,
either directly or indirectly. The intent of the author is only to offer
information of a general nature to help you in your quest for emotional
and spiritual well-being. In the event you use any of the information
in this book for yourself, which is your constitutional right, the
author and the publisher assume no responsibility for your actions.*

*Any people depicted in stock imagery provided by Thinkstock are
models, and such images are being used for illustrative purposes only.
Certain stock imagery © Thinkstock.*

*ISBN: 978-1-4525-3739-9 (sc)
ISBN: 978-1-4525-3738-2 (e)*

Library of Congress Control Number: 2011914014

Printed in the United States of America

Balboa Press rev. date: 8/9/2011

CONTENTS

GRATITUDE ACKNOWLEDGEMENT

I give my heartfelt thanks to God for walking beside me on my journey and I also would like to thank my husband Stefan, and my children Tom, Kevin and Waylon for blessing me with more love and joy than I could ever expected in life.

A LETTER FROM ME TO YOU

To my dearest readers,

Our lives consist solely on choices we make everyday. We choose to be positive or negative, have a good day or bad, approve or disapprove, accept or deny, be encouraged or discouraged, be happy or sad, feel power or powerless, be successful or a failure, and in my mind one of the most important is to believe in the unseen or disbelieve in your ability to achieve your dreams. Every day of our lives we encounter circumstances that can change our attitudes, but it is completely up to us how we choose to be affected by the events.

I would like to thank you for choosing to read my book, and giving me the chance to help guide you on your inspirational journey to self-fulfillment and abundance. I'm sure there have been times when you found yourself in situations that seem to have no light at the end of the tunnel, and perhaps at this very moment you are experiencing one of those situations. I want to re-assure you that there will always be light to follow darkness. I know firsthand what it's like to experience financial burdens, depression, divorce, sexual abuse, and other miserable circumstances. My faith has been tested beyond immense measures in my life. I've rode raging rivers and had to climb mountains that had rockslides, but

I always prayed that the absolute best outcome would be delivered to me when the situation ended. I realized since I started my inspirational journey that every thing that I've endured in life has had a purpose. I am a stronger, wiser and more spiritual being from all my experiences. We all have a life story, and every life story has a meaning.

Have you ever imagined living your life in complete tranquility? The kind of life where you thought your dreams only existed over the rainbow. It's possible to change the way you currently know your existence to a more meaningful and exhilarating life. Your life is your own investment, and I firmly believe that if you dislike the color of your life, then you have to paint it a different shade. You need to be an artist and make your life your masterpiece. You aren't restricted to just white or black. You have an enormous array of colors to choose from in life, and the only thing that would be holding you back from coloring your life is the fear of the unknown or fear of change.

For the first time in your life, why not create your own rainbow and let it lead you to the pot of gold. Let the colors of your rainbow represent peace, harmony, abundance of health, prosperity, faith and well-being for your spirit.

In 2002, I started on my journey to balancing and enriching my life. My first introduction to viewing life from a different perspective was Feng Shui. Feng Shui is the ancient Chinese art of promoting and balancing health, wealth, and happiness by harnessing positive energy from your environment. I was amazed and captivated by this art of living, which has ultimately led me to studying how the field of energy in the universe can modify each and everyone of our lives to its fullest potential.

A few years after I started studying about the fields of positive and negative energy a book called "The Secret" hit the market. The Secret confirmed everything I've been studying, but I realized it was only the tip of the iceberg. I've read some fascinating books from authors like Dr. Wayne Dyer, Deepak Chopra, Lillian Too, and Rick Warren, which opened up new and exciting adventures for me. Tapping into the power of energy has evolved my life, and I'm sure it will eventually transform your life beyond your wildest dreams too.

The field of energy surrounds us and resides within every one of us. There is positive and negative energy, and how you choose to make use of the energy is completely up to you. There are so many people in the world who want to change their existing circumstances, but they don't know how to do it. They don't realize that the way they are thinking and speaking is how their lives are playing out— like a soap opera, which is full of drama, chaos, sadness, and desperation. I've seen this way of living everyday of my life.

My husband and I owned a small country tavern for almost 5 years, and I've met customers who lived a life of misery with a black cloud above their heads. Their negative thoughts appeared to be set on auto-pilot. Their destructive way of thinking had become their way of life; they had created their own self-fulfilling prophecy, to live a life of sorrow and misfortune. I believe in a higher supreme power, a Creator, which I call God, and God didn't create us to be miserable. Our Creator wants us to live a glorious life and rejoice, because He is present and alive in each and every person. He is a part of our inner Spirit.

I've been examining the effects of how people publicly speak to one another for the past several years and I've come to the conclusion that all negative conversations create negative outcomes. I witnessed one of my customers who spoke about cancer in almost every conversation and the cancer eventually became her reality. She was diagnosed with cancer about a year after her constant bleak conversations with other people and she passed away shortly after her diagnosis. I've watched some of the most heart-wrenching stories come into reality from the way people constantly talked about negative things. I've learned a great deal about people and how their negative behavior came into existence just from the way they spoke on a daily basis. When you speak negatively that means you're constantly thinking about negativity.

My inner voice has been urging me to write this book about harnessing positive energy and how you can create your deepest desires into reality. I want everyone to realize that they can turn their thoughts around and invent a new way of living for themselves.

I will be truthful and let you know right up front that your journey may start out very slowly. It would be awesome if tomorrow your life was exactly the way you wished it to be, but in reality this process will take some time. The change in your life will depend on your determination to shift your thoughts from being negative to positive. There's no magical genie that can grant your desires, because you hold the power to shift your life. I intend to guide you on how to turn your preconditioned thoughts around, so you can manifest the supreme life that God gave you when you were born. Your mind is so powerful and you'll begin your journey by learning how to clear all the constant negative clutter that has been holding you back from claiming your true happiness. You will need to treat your negative thoughts with firm, direct discipline. When those negative thoughts start to chatter in your mind, tell them to "BE QUIET!" You're in control of your thoughts, so believe in yourself and stay positive. Your goal is to shift your thoughts around which will enable you to achieve all that you wish to become your reality.

First of all, be patient with yourself, and you will soon see your thoughts moving toward a brighter horizon. Dr. Wayne Dyer eloquently states in his book "The Power of

Intention," *"change the way you look at things and things change the way they look."* What an incredible instruction given by Dr. Dyer. If we all lived with just that one quote in our minds, we would find a lot more opportunities knocking on our doors and silver linings in what we thought were undesirable circumstances. All circumstances have a purpose and capturing the knowledge from the situations will be a useful tool in your life. You may not immediately know why you're being challenged in life, but someday you'll receive the answer.

I'm confident that after you've read this book, you will have taken your first step to a new beginning and profound chapter in your life.

I look forward to sharing my experiences with you in this book, and always remember as you are reading that I am here in spirit with you.

As my four-year-old son would say, "Happy travels to you."

All my love and abundant blessings to you,

Barbara

CHAPTER ONE

"KEEPING FAITH"
BELIEVE

The hidden fortune within your mind and beyond is a buried treasure that exists within you. You hold the secret treasure abundantly filled with brilliant jewels, and now it's time for you to find the key to unlocking it. The sky is the limit with endless possibilities for what you so desire in your life. You're only as successful as your dreams and your dreams are only as successful as your POWER to BELIEVE in them. Your hidden fortune is as authentic as the sun rising and setting before your eyes everyday. You are the one and only master that holds the golden key that can open your buried treasure.

Your mind set is the first step to changing the world around you. What you think, speak and believe to be true in your life is what your world shall be. As I mentioned in the introduction, it will take time for you to recondition your thoughts, so please do not give up on yourself. Open your mind and heart to what can change your life.

As I started to write this book, I can honestly say that I asked my Creator to guide me with each chapter and speak to me through my inner spirit. My first experience with His assistance was this very chapter that I'm writing now. I was sitting here at my computer and wasn't sure what to say or how to start my first chapter. I was at a loss before I even began. I asked God for his guidance. Within a minute, I heard a crash in my bedroom. My four-year-old son and I went in there, because I thought one of my cats had broken something. I looked around and at first didn't see anything out of place, then glanced over by the window next to my bed and saw a small glass window chime on the floor. The window chime had been hanging in that window for about seven years. The chime has never fallen down and I even forgot that it was there. Bending down to pick up the chime, I was completely amazed that God brought me the first answer that I was looking for. The chime says, *"Faith is . . . The substance of things hoped for . . . the evidence of things unseen, without faith, we can do nothing . . . with faith, all things are possible."* I immediately knew that "Keeping Faith" was the first chapter in my book. There was a second message sent to me through a facebook application, which is called "God wants you to know." I received a message which confirmed that God was speaking to me through signs within my home. The message said, "Faith is exactly what it takes to get through uncertainty. Faith is not necessary when you know how things are going to work out,—that's knowledge. It's in the time of unknowing that having faith sees you through to the other side. Faith is what gives you strength. Faith is that light in your heart that keeps on shining even when it's all darkness outside. Now is the time to keep that faith alive!" Thank you God for the prompt answer!

If you truly want to create the best possible life for yourself, then you need to make a vow to yourself right at this moment in time that you intend to stay positive every day. You have to BELIEVE in abundance, ACHIEVE your abundance and then you'll RECEIVE abundance. These three words seem so simple, but they are so powerful and greatly beneficial to you. You must first BELIEVE that keeping faith in all that is unseen will give birth to all your desires. You are a profound and unique being. You have senses that allow you to touch, see, taste, hear and smell. You being blessed with these senses should give you enough faith to believe that all things are possible. You are blessed with these senses for a reason, and unfortunately many of us take them for granted.

Take a few moments and look out your window at nature. I'm serious, I want you to open your eyes and see the beauty that surrounds you. We have a tendency to take for granted the magnificent sights of golden sunrises peeking over the horizon, sunsets with glorious hues of orange and purple flowing across the sky, birds gracefully flying and singing, flowers blooming that have vibrant colors and sweet fragrant scents, the array of brilliant colors decorating the trees in the fall, and fresh blankets of white glistening snow across the land in the winter. The visual appearance of nature is also a potent source of reassurance that all things are possible. So, when you have doubts about your faith in the unseen, and the unseen becoming your reality, just take a good look around at nature. God created the most beautiful and serene visions for us to enjoy in our lives.

Another great reassurance factor is the advanced technology that surrounds you. Have you ever given thanks for being blessed with electricity, hot water, indoor plumbing, a refrigerator, stove, dishwasher, cell phone, camera, air conditioning, television, computer, or a washer and dryer? These amenities were designed and built by people. These people believed in the evidence of things unseen and made them a part of your reality.

Have you ever heard of the Law of Nature, the Law of the Universe, or the Law of Attraction? All three of these laws are the basic nature of God's laws. In simple terms, whatever you give out, God will eventually give back to you. The Bible says, "Give, and it shall be given to you." Luke 6:37-38. This is not a new concept of thinking; it has been around for thousands of years.

In my business, I communicate with people on a daily basis. One of the customers; Dennis has overwhelming negative thoughts. He is such a kind-hearted man, but continuously states that nothing of beneficial value ever comes to him in life, and it's worthless to even try and think in a positive manner. My response to him was, "you just fulfilled another negative intention in your life and so now it shall be your reality." The Law of Nature will ALWAYS give you what you think and speak about. I'm sure you've heard the quote; "you reap what you sow." This is so true! " . . . He which soweth sparingly shall reap also sparingly; and he which soweth bountifully shall reap also bountifully." 2 Corinthians 9:6. If you plant a positive or negative thought in your mind, eventually the thought grows into reality. It's no different than planting seeds in a garden and within a couple of weeks they start to flourish into flowers or vegetables. It's unfortunate that most people in the world go through life with the saying, "I'll believe it when I see it."

If you want to change the circumstances in your life, you have to stay on track with your intentions. Deviating from your intentions only brings more negative thoughts to the surface and into your reality. I know you have the potential to accomplish all that you desire in your life, because we were all created from the same Source. Imagine that your life is a playing field for a sports team. There are two teams in the game. You are on the Positive Patriots and the opposing team is called the Negative Ninjas. You know, just like in any sports game, there is only one team that can win. The dominating team has the stronger, more driven, assertive and aspiring players. You are the MVP (most valued player) for your team. In your game which is your life, you must choose who will be a part of your team. You want to attract and reinforce your team with players who are positive thinkers just like you. If for some reason, one of your players along the way starts to stray from your corner, you'll want to eliminate him/her from your team. You must associate yourself with people who are attracting the same positive essence that you are aiming to achieve in life. When you have people who condemn your positive thoughts and words, they are influencing your thoughts with doubt, fear and negativity. Their negativity also sends signals of resisting energy into your life.

One of the absolute best things you can do for yourself and your journey to creating a new life for yourself is to write in a journal. I'm not the first or the last person who will tell you how important it is to write your thoughts, desires and blessings down on paper. Your journal will express your everyday blessings that you are truly thankful for in life. Your journal can exhibit all your wishes and desires. It is in your best interest to keep your journal private, because not everyone will believe in your willpower to manifest abundance coming into your life. You must have an open mind and heart in order to believe that you can bring an abundance of joy, health and prosperity into your life. I know for a fact that not all people believe in this power of creation. I have personally shared thoughts with some of my customers about using positive energy to exhibit an outcome for a personal situation, and they laughed at me with disbelief. For some people, it's difficult to imagine the unseen. It is either black or white. Another part that is really wondrous about journaling is that you can go back and physically see what you've written and when it became part of your reality. So, put dates on your pages when you're journaling.

When I first started journaling my blessings, I found it to be a little mundane and not as fulfilling for me, so I decided to write letters to God about what I was grateful for in my life. I find that when I write an actual letter, I experience a deeper sensation of heartfelt gratitude. When I engage my inner-self with heartfelt gratitude, there is a peaceful awareness that fills my spirit. I recommend that you do whatever feels right for you and perhaps you will have a different way to journal your blessings. This is just a thought for you, but maybe you could be creative and decorate a box and fill it each day with notes that contain your heartfelt dedications.

It's also important before you go to sleep at night to leave your worries to God and thank Him for what already exists in your life. You may think this sounds a little strange, but when you believe that God is in your corner, your fears will dissolve. If you are experiencing a downfall in your life, I will stress that you keep your faith alive and believe that God is standing by your side. When you wake up in the morning, you should always give thanks to Him for giving you another day to change your life. Everyday that you are alive, you are receiving a gift from Him and your gift is your life. You're being blessed with unlimited potential to be one step closer to your dreams. Each morning start your day by declaring that you'll have an absolutely fabulous day. The more you consistently proclaim this statement; you will be living a magnificent life. Every day say the positive affirmation, "I make a difference and I make it happen."

If you think you have boundaries in your life, it's because the negative chatter in your mind is creating those boundaries for you. Whatever you think is what you believe. If you're stuck in a rut with your life, when you wake up in the morning imagine that today is the beginning of your new life and that EVERYTHING IS POSSIBLE. You should never ever give up on yourself and your faith in the unseen. If you give up, then you ultimately are giving up on your unlimited potential and purpose in life. You were born for a reason and I guarantee you that God has a superb plan for you. Each and every one of us living on this earth has a purpose to be alive.

Are you wondering and questioning now what your purpose in life is? Okay, if you question your purpose, then you probably don't have something you are passionate about. If this happens to be the case for you, then you should start by making *your life your passion*. Dedicate each day to fulfilling your life with an abundance of joy. When you get up in the morning, smile at the world and look at yourself in the mirror and say "I am a shining star." Don't let another day pass you by without driving yourself to become a happier person. Your happiness is a part of who you are and not to be found from an outside source. There is no drug or person who can create your profound joy. When you feel the excitement that drives your life, you will then be content with the way you are living your life. The overflowing passion in your life will lead to opening the doors to your unseen objects or opportunities. Your faith will always play an enormous role, because if you doubt for one second that your current life won't change, then you are right back where you started. When you need a little pick me up in your day play some upbeat music like "Stayin' Alive" by the Bee Gees and dance and sing, until you feel the passion of joy fill your whole body.

I've observed people for years and how they threw themselves a "pity party" and couldn't understand why their lives were miserable. They say they want to change their current existence, but they won't put forth the effort in changing their negative thinking patterns. For me, I view the outcome of destructive thinking to driving your vehicle down the wrong side of the road into oncoming traffic. Now you know that there will be a collision and depending on the impact of the crash, it could be fatal to someone in the accident. Your negative thoughts are exactly parallel to oncoming traffic. When your negative thoughts rule your life, you succumb to constant battles and disasters in whatever you do.

7

Barbara Brusky

I want you to understand how important it is to stay on track with your positive thoughts and keeping faith in the unseen. You and only you can transform your life.

I want everyone in this world to experience a surplus of pleasure in their lives. I wish I could snap my fingers and create a world of people filled with everything they desire in their lives, but I know that my purpose is to guide as many people as I can to achieving their dreams. I can guide you through examples of situations that I've experienced and the lessons I've learned in my life. I can also guide you with the knowledge I've acquired through situations that I've seen other people encounter in their lives.

Everyday you will be taking a baby step toward unlocking your hidden treasures. You will be able to defeat any obstacles in your life by holding on to your faith. You will be able to achieve your deepest desires when you stay on track with your positive thoughts. Believing in you and keeping faith in the unseen is a life long process. It's no different than feeding your body with food and water to stay alive. You have to keep nourishing your thoughts with positive affirmations if you want them to stay alive.

I'm going to share a personal story with you that consumed my entire being, which led me to being angry, depressed, sad and feeling hopeless, until one day I just surrendered my problem to God and I chose to rise above the stormy situation in my life, and feel the warmth of God's love embrace me.

Five years ago my husband and I purchased our tavern, and I never thought that when the time came to sell it, we would encounter any issues. Approximately a year and half ago, I decided to aggressively dedicate my time to finding a buyer for our business. We had interested parties, and I felt we could sell the business within six months. In April 2010, a lady inquired about purchasing the tavern and we agreed on a $10,000.00 down payment and then monthly installments, until the business was paid in full. My husband and I had a final fare-well party at our tavern with our customers, and I was truly relieved to be done working the long 17 hour shifts in our business. Two weeks after we thought our tavern was sold, I received a phone call from Elizabeth who was supposed to purchase the tavern. She told me that she decided to purchase the café right next door to our business, and that she no longer had any interest in the tavern. Okay, I felt a little disheartened, but I knew God would bring the right person to take over our bar the "Ironhorse Saloon." Within a couple of weeks we had a few more interested parties who were very serious about buying the business; we explained to them that they needed to meet with the landlord who owned the strip mall where our business was located. As a formality to changing the lease from our name to the new owner, everyone had to speak to the landlord. Each of these perspective buyers called and met with the landlord, but to my surprise the landlord decided he wouldn't let my husband and I out of our lease, which didn't end for another 10 months. I was completely dumbfounded. I cried for days and was literally so physically sick that I could barely function with my daily routine. Our contract clearly stated that the landlord would not be unreasonable when we decided to sell the business. After a couple of days of being in complete shock, I had to think outside of the box for an answer to this problem, because we could no longer sustain the time and money to keep the business open. My husband had a full-time job now, and I needed to be home to care for our children. One morning I asked Stefan if we should just let one of the perspective buyers take over our business and pray that at the end of the ten months, we could transfer the lease into his name and finally be able to sell the tavern to him. Stefan thought that was a great idea and he called Keith to see if he was interested in taking control of the tavern for the next ten months. Keith said "yes" and my husband and I thought we could finally put this dramatic situation behind us. In March 2011, I retained a contractual attorney for the business, because the landlord had signed our premises over to Elizabeth, who purchased the café next door to our business. Apparently, the landlord had no intention of letting my husband and I sell our tavern, because he signed a four year contract with Elizabeth back in June 2010, to take over our premises when our lease ended. The landlord interfered with the sale of our business, but in order for us to sue him; we would have to retain a litigation attorney now. There was no guarantee that we would win the lawsuit, so I chose to surrender this predicament to God. We lost $150,000.00, which was what we originally paid for the tavern and another $50,000.00 for start up costs and full restoration of the business.

I believe there was a purpose for my husband and I to have experienced this awful and bizarre circumstance. My faith is the one and only thing I knew I could rely on to guide me through to a peaceful ending for such a tumultuous problem. I thank God for being here for me, and letting me relinquish this burden to him. It is my faith and belief in a Supreme Power that gives me strength, courage, comfort and security that there will be another way for my husband and me to recuperate our financial losses.

If you find yourself with a problem that you can no longer carry on your shoulders, I found this perfect intention for starting your day and it's a title of a book written by Joyce Meyer.

> *Good Morning!*
> *This is God.*
> *I will be handling*
> *all of your problems today.*
> *I will not need your help,*
> *so have a good day.*
> *I Love You!*

You just received your first lesson in "The Hidden Fortune within the Mind & Beyond." Now, you'll learn about how to achieve your hidden fortunes in chapter two.

CHAPTER TWO

METHODS TO ACHIEVING ABUNDANCE

I love this chapter, because there are so many different ways you can achieve the abundance you are seeking in your life. Are you searching for love, wealth, health, influential people or good friends? Perhaps, you wish to fulfill one or all of these areas in your life. If so, then you have a great deal of choices to achieving what you yearn for in life. I think the best part about achieving your abundance is that you can utilize every method to benefit you. I believe these methods to achieving abundance are gifts for us. These gifts stand for Gods Inspiration For Total Serenity.

Each method is a different avenue for you to choose from to assist in changing your inner well-being. In order to shift what's happening in your outer world, you have to transform what you believe to be true for your inner self.

MEDITATION

My favorite method to achieving abundance is Meditation. According to Webster's Dictionary, "meditation is a discourse intended to express its author's reflections or to guide other's in contemplation." Meditation is considered to be a way of entering into the quiet place in your mind and assist you in centering yourself toward inner peace. Meditation is an inspiring way for you to enhance your skills in keeping your faith in the unseen. It is a guided way to spiritual enlightenment. Meditation is a form of therapy to achieving a healthy mind, body and soul. The benefits of meditating are incredible and rejuvenating.

Remember back in the first chapter when I spoke about positive and negative energy. Your body is composed of energy and in meditation you learn about Chakra's that are aligned in the center of your body. When your Chakra's are open and balanced, the energy flows effortlessly through your body. When one or more of your Chakra's are obstructed that correlates to the energy in your body being blocked.

We have seven major chakras in our body. Every chakra is associated with a color, a stone, one of the five senses or an internal system, and a principle. The Base or Root Chakra is located at the lower tip of your spinal column. The Root Chakra is associated with human survival and security. It is the chakra that keeps you grounded to the earth. The second chakra is located in the pelvic region and it's associated with family and male/female sexuality. The third chakra is located right above the naval, which is called the solar plexus chakra. This chakra is identified with personal empowerment; it's your will to create your dreams. The fourth chakra is in the area of your heart and it correlates to love and faith. The fifth chakra is located in the throat, where creative expression, communication, abundance and manifestation are located. The sixth chakra which is also known as the "third eye" is situated right in between your eyebrows; it's associated with your intuition and spiritual awareness. The last chakra is known as the crown and it's located at the very top of your head, and is related to universal consciousness.

I enjoy listening to meditation music, because it soothes my body and soul. I found an incredible CD called Chakra Balancing: Body, Mind and Soul by Deepak Chopra and I would highly recommend it to you, if you're thinking about trying meditation.

There is so much to learn about meditation and if you're interested in expanding your knowledge about "how to meditate," you should go to the website *www.chopra.com*. I've read some interesting books written by Mr. Chopra and they are truly amazing pieces of work. He is not only a renowned author, but he specializes in meditation.

Besides listening to music, I also use a deck of meditation cards. The cards give detailed information for visualizing abundance, inner peace, health, creativity, wisdom, inspiration, and many more beneficial exercises which assist in creating harmony in someone's' life.

VISUALIZATION

Visualization is another method to achieving your abundance. This technique uses your imagination to create the unseen objects and opportunities that you are seeking in your life. Before you go to sleep at night, visualize your dreams becoming your reality. When you are in unison with the positive wave length of the cosmos or universe, you will be able to tap into your dreams. Visualization will also work for you during the day. As you think about what you want in your life, you should visualize it around you. You can visualize romance, money, joy, health, wisdom, friendships or any type of object. When you visualize your dream, you need to keep the faith and believe what you want to achieve. The process of visualizing your dream comes from within the power of your mind. For instance, if you want money to flow effortlessly into your pockets, then you can't let fear overwhelm your thoughts. You have this dream, but you're thinking that the bills are overdue, so how in the world are you suppose to come up with the money to pay them. Well, if you have a tendency to think about the shortage of money to pay the bills, then fear overshadows your dream. Your reality stays the same, because you let the negative power win.

Remember; tell the negative to Keep Quiet! Those thoughts aren't welcome in your mind. The technique of visualizing only works when you wholeheartedly believe in the unseen. If you can let go of any doubt you may have toward attaining what you would like to have in your life, one day you will see that you've created a whole new life for yourself.

Here's an example of how I visualized one of my dreams becoming my reality, during the day: About seven years ago, every time the song the "Christmas Cannon" played on the radio, I would imagine myself walking down the aisle and being united in matrimony to my boyfriend Stefan. I would slowly walk around my kitchen and living room, tears of love rolling down my cheeks and holding an imaginary bouquet of flowers. I completely believed that I was marrying Stefan. Stefan and I never spoke about getting married, but during the summer of 2005, we were married in a little white chapel in Las Vegas with the music "the Wedding Cannon" playing in the background.

We all have the capability within our powerful minds to create anything that we wish to become a part of our reality. We just have to believe in the unseen.

It's also important on your journey to visualizing your new life, you have to let go of being jealous and envious of other people, and what they have in their lives. If you find yourself being envious, you've disrupted the positive energy flow for your dreams. You let envy detach you from your dream. It's important to stay positive and be happy for what other people have acquired in their lives.

PRESENTATION OF SELF AND YOUR INNER SPIRIT

This technique derives from how you think, speak and act towards others. I believe true beauty lies within the heart and soul of the beholder. How do you treat people, animals, nature and the world that surrounds you? Whatever you do to others is what is done to you. This is the "ethic of reciprocity" and your Karma. According to Answers.com, "Karma is the total effect of a person's actions and conduct during the successive phases of the person's existence, regarded as determining the person's destiny." The "ethic of reciprocity" according to Wikipedia is "more commonly known as the Golden Rule, which is an ethical code that states one has a right to just treatment, and a responsibility to ensure justice for others. A key element of the golden rule is that a person attempting to live by this rule treats all people, not just members of his or her in-group, with consideration." The "ethic of reciprocity" is known around the world in various cultures and religions. The philosophy has the same principle meaning for Buddhism, Christianity, Confucianism, Hinduism, Islam, Judaism and Taoism. Here are some quotes from various religions:

* "Therefore all things whatsoever ye would that men should do to you, do ye even so to them: for this is the law and the prophets." Matthew 7:12 ~ Christianity
* "Never impose on others what you would not choose for yourself." Confucius, Analects XV.24 (tr. David Hinton) ~ Confucianism
* "Hurt no one so that no one may hurt you." Muhammad, The Farewell Sermon ~ Islam
* "One should never do that to another which one regards as injurious to one's own self. This, in brief, is the rule of dharma." Brihaspati Mahabharata (Anusasana Parva. Section CXIII. Verse 8) ~ Hinduism
* "You shall not take vengeance or bear a grudge against your countrymen. Love your fellow as yourself: I am the LORD." Leviticus 19:18 ~ Judaism
* "The truly enlightened ones are those who neither incite fear in others nor fear anyone themselves." P.1427, Slok, Guru Granth Sahib (tr. Patwant Singh) ~ Sikhism and Karma

All people have room in their lives for self improvement, and the one question that has perplexed me for most of my adult life is "Why do people criticize, judge, gossip, control, belittle and verbally/emotionally abuse other people?" We all have a life of our own to live, and if we are living our lives to our fullest potential, we wouldn't have time to become negatively involved in someone else's life. Every negative thing you think, speak or act out towards someone else will come back to haunt you; you're damaging your life. This behavior was not our Creators intention for us. The choices you make in your life will create your Karma. When you choose to think, speak or act with negative implications towards someone, you're setting into motion the effect that it will have on you. If you don't like the way your life is right now, then it's time for you to set yourself free from the negative shackles that have become your anchor to achieving your dreams. The key to setting yourself free from the negative shackles is to be positive. You'll find freedom, when you're spirit is soaring with positive influences you instill on yourself and on everyone who surrounds you, including nature.

SPIRITUALISM ~ signs from angels

Do you believe in Angels? I'm talking about a spiritual being superior to man; like a loved one who has passed away. The technique of spiritualism is unique, because your angels are giving you signs in life to help guide and comfort you on your path. Do you think that the things that happen to you or even the people that you meet in your life are just by random chance? I would like to share a few short stories with you that happened to me, in my life. These stories are concrete evidence to me that Angels are watching over us.

Short Story 1

When I was 18, I went on vacation with my best friend and her family to Rhinelander Wisconsin. We stayed at a resort and one evening my best friend and I went with another girl from the resort to visit some of her friends that lived in another town about 45 minutes away. When we decided to drive back to Rhinelander, it was raining and around 10 o'clock at night. In northern Wisconsin, there are no street lights in the country and its terrain is described as a thick dense forest of pine trees. We were in the middle of nowhere, when the girl that was driving lost control of the vehicle around a curve, in the road. Our car hydro-planed on the wet pavement and then flipped over several times. When the vehicle came to a stop, it was upside down and in a swampy area of the forest. We managed to get out of the car, and it was pitch black outside. We were a bit disoriented and none of us were sure of where the road was located. After we found the road, we started walking. As God as my witness, it was probably a few minutes later and all of the sudden an elderly couple driving in their car found us. The couple stopped to pick us up and when we asked them to drop us off at the house that we had just left, they happened to live right next door to that home! The odds of someone finding us in the middle of nowhere are pretty phenomenal, but when these people lived next door to the home we were just at is like winning a multi-million dollar jackpot in the lottery. That was my very first realization that Angels exist in this world.

Short Story 2

Seven years ago, I had a very endearing experience. I took my grandfather into **m**y home because he was dying from bladder cancer. I have a hillside home, and the lower level of my home is like an apartment. My grandfather loved it, because he felt like he was still living on his own, but he had the love of his family surrounding him. Grandpa only lived with me for six months before he passed away. During the last weeks of his life, there was a day when I found him crying like a child in a fetal position. I thought maybe he had a nightmare, because he kept telling me "to get everyone out of his bedroom." I told him, "grandpa we are the only two people in the room." He went on to tell me that his deceased wife Ginny, his deceased brother Lyle and several other deceased people were standing around his bed. My grandfathers Angels were in his bedroom and calling him home to heaven. I prayed to the Lord to set my grandfathers soul free before Christmas. I wrote a poem to God and expressed my emotions to Him. The poem is called, "He Wants to Be with You," and I would like to share it with you.

Life is a journey,
Which road shall I take?
Lord please guide me,
What decisions should I make?
I've chosen a road, which is difficult to tread.
I try not to complain,
I turn to you Lord, instead.
My grandfather is dying
He is terminally ill.
Stop his body from crying
For he has made a wish, only you can fulfill.
He lives in pain
And that's no way to "Be."
Just take him away Lord
And set his soul free.
My grandfather is so loving and tender,
Please Lord,
Let his body surrender.
I've given him all my love
And did all that I can do.
He no longer needs me Lord,
Since he wants to be with you.

On December 22, an extremely cold and snowy night in Wisconsin, my grandfather passed away. My family and I were downstairs, when the funeral home came to pick him up around 9 o'clock at night. There's a sliding glass door downstairs, and we started hearing this constant tapping on it. My husband opened the blinds and to our surprise there was a small sparrow pecking at the window. I knew in my heart that it was my grandfather and he was letting us know that his soul was set free. In the Gospel of Matthew in the Bible, there's a passage that God describes about the sparrow. The meaning of the passage is best described in the song, "His Eye Is on the Sparrow." Civilla Martin, who wrote the lyrics, said this about her inspiration to write the song based on the scripture of Matthew. "Early in the spring of 1905, my husband and I were sojourning in Elmira, New York. We contracted a deep friendship for a couple by the name of Mr. and Mrs. Doolittle—true saints of God. Mrs. Doolittle had been bedridden for twenty years. Her husband was crippled and had to propel himself to and from his business in a wheel chair. Despite their afflictions, they lived happy Christian lives, bringing inspiration and comfort to all who knew them. One day while we were visiting with the Doolittle's, my husband commented on their bright hopefulness and asked them for the secret of it. Mrs. Doolittle's reply was simple: "His eye is on the sparrow, and I know He watches me." The beauty of this simple expression of boundless faith gripped the hearts and fired the imagination of Dr. Martin and me. The hymn "His Eye Is on the Sparrow" was the outcome of that experience."

Short Story 3

On March 31, 2010, my step-mother unexpectedly passed away from a heart attack. My brother Donny and his wife Tricia live in Florida, so they came home for mom's funeral. My sister-in-law Tricia is a very spiritual woman just like I am.

The day before they went back to their home in Florida, I found an Angel's web site posted on my facebook page. I printed out the 22 pages, which described number sequences and how repetitious numbers are signs from Angels. Tricia asked me if she could take the pages I had printed out. I said sure and the next day, I just printed out another copy for myself. After I printed these pages, I didn't have to time to read them, since I had to go to work at our business. While I was at work, I started wiping the bar rails, and I found a penny. I just put it in my back pocket and didn't think anything about it. Later that day, I started finding pennies and dimes everywhere. I was being showered with pennies and dimes every where I went. It seemed quite strange to me, since there was such an abundance of them. When I went to the gas station, I found a penny and dime on the ground. In the afternoon, I was separating clothes to do the laundry, and when I picked a shirt off the floor, there were five pennies and five dimes underneath it.

In the evening, I finally had a chance to sit down and read those pages I printed out about the Angel number sequences. As I was reading, there was a post on page 18 which said "finding pennies or dimes are messages from our deceased loved ones telling us they are fine." Wow, wow, wow, I was surprised and realized these were signs from my mother. I felt completely at peace knowing that she was in heaven and there was nothing to worry about.

We are deeply blessed to have Guardian Angels to watch over us, but most people aren't aware of their presence and the signs they bestow upon us. Signs from Angels come in all sorts of forms. Signs can be found in cloud formations, animals, birds, Bible quotations, repetitious numbers, songs, people, rainbows and fragrances. I can even remember when my grandfather was living with me; there were three occasions where I could smell my grandmother's perfume in one of the bathrooms. I knew that my grandmother was present in my home.

There are specific reasons for things to occur in our lives and it's not just by coincidence. There is a purpose for why I was inspired to write this book, and there is a purpose for you to be reading it. There is a greater power which exists above and beyond our known world. It is up to you to let your faith guide you to the answers you are searching for in life. When you pray or ask questions, then pay attention to your surroundings for signs that will lead you to your answers. While I was writing this book, I stumbled upon a spiritual writer and her name is Doreen Virtue. I checked out her website *www.beliefnet.com/ Inspiration/Angels*, and if you're interested in furthering your knowledge about Angels, I suggest you take a look at this site or purchase one of her books.

Every aspect of this book always returns back to keeping your faith in the unseen and believing that everything is possible in your life.

MENTAL APPLICATION

In this final method, you retrain your mental activity that you constantly think about on a day to day basis. You're an optimist or pessimist. You're a complainer or achiever. You can't be both. If you're an optimist, you believe that the best possible outcome will always happen from any situation. If you're a pessimist, you think of the most unfavorable outcome for any situation. You can't see the silver-lining or opportunities that lie ahead of you when you experience a negative predicament.

If you make your life your passion, you will be surprised how the negative thoughts start to disappear from your mind. If you're thinking that you've tried this approach and it didn't work for you, then you've let your own negative thoughts become your ball and chain holding you in the lifestyle that you're currently living.

I'm going to give you a list for people who are complainers and achievers and then you decide which category best describes the person you are.

COMPLAINER	ACHIEVER
1. There are no jobs on the market.	I will find a job.
2. That job is too far for me to drive to.	I enjoy the extra time for me.
3. I don't want to work over-time.	I have more spending money.
4. The rich only get richer.	I'm filling the abundance in my life.
5. Life isn't fair.	I'll find a key to open the next door.
6. I live pay check to pay check.	I'll find a part-time job for extra cash
7. I'm not going back to school.	I'm enhancing my knowledge.
8. I lost my job.	What's my next opportunity?
9. I hate exercising.	Thank God I'm not handicapped.
10. I never win.	I'm a magnet for prosperity.

Okay, did you find yourself under the list of complainers? If you did, then you need to change these fatalistic words of "I can't, I won't, I'm not and I hate," to "I can, I will, I am and I love." Your life is a canvas of possibilities, and you have the power within your mind to change the pattern of your thoughts. When you become consciously aware of your thoughts, you will be able to alter your thoughts with positive affirmations. Today is the perfect day for you to start applying the achievers affirmations in your thoughts. If you choose not to alter your thoughts, then the outcome of tomorrow will be exactly as last month, last week, yesterday and today. You are the direct cause to the consequences that affect your life. It's no different than if you chose to hit yourself with a hammer and you'll feel instant pain. It's not a gratifying outcome to

23

what you chose to do to yourself. This is exactly what your thoughts are doing to you; you're not achieving a gratifying outcome in your life. If you've been the type of person who thought, "If I didn't have bad luck, I wouldn't have any luck at all," then today is the time to replace that thought too! Truthfully, I don't believe in bad luck.

When I first started altering my thoughts, I placed images around my home to remind myself of what I wanted to achieve in my life. I was determined to get rid of my "destructive" thoughts that were invading my mind space and replace them with the harmony and prosperity I wanted to create for my reality. I like to think of these images as my "visionary mirror." What ever I cut out of magazines or objects that I use to decorate my home with, I see them as a mirror of my life. They are what my heart yearns for and what I want to attract into my life. To give you an idea of what I'm talking about, I will share some of the examples I placed around my home which enabled me to change my thoughts and attract more of what my heart wanted.

1. I had to stop thinking about certain people that constantly complained around me, so I cut words out of a magazine that said, "I want more inspiring and good friends." I placed a photo of my friend Steve who lives in Las Vegas next to these words to remind myself of the type of people I wanted in my life. It was a way for me to disconnect myself from the negative thoughts I had from people who irritated me. The photograph and words also connected me with a higher energy level that attracted more inspiring people into my life.
2. I wanted to stop thinking about not having enough money, so I took one of my Jade trees and created a money tree out of it. I took currency and made little Chinese fans out of them and then attached

the money to the Jade leaves with paper clips. Now I have my very own money tree. I also placed a sailing ship on my fireplace hearth, which is adorned with money from around the world. The sailing ship is one of the ways I applied Feng Shui to enhance my mental shift of thoughts. This visual technique has worked quite well for my husband's business. He consistently receives orders from around the world on a weekly basis.

3. I wanted to learn how to enter the quiet area of my mind, so I would stop thinking about useless information that was blocking my path to abundance. I cut out a woman from a magazine, who was meditating. This image brought opportunities to me that would help me learn different techniques for meditating. Example: On my facebook page, I found an invitation to join a group for Japa Meditation. Japa Meditation is reciting the repetition of a mantra. A mantra is not just words; it is a manifestation of God in the form of sounds like Ahh. Japa meditation is wonderful, because you can practice it any time of day when you have a few spare minutes. Prior to this invitation, I never heard of Japa Meditation.

GODS INSPIRATION FOR TOTAL SERENITY = GIFTS

These methods for achieving abundance are like inspirational gifts, which are the foundation to your healthy inner self or spirit. Through meditation, visualization, presentation of self, spiritualism and mental application, you're decluttering and reorganizing your thoughts for fulfilling your dreams. If you want to attain power, then you have to let go of fear. If you want to attain prosperity, then you have to let go of the absence of money. If you want to attain love, then you have to let go of hate. If you

Barbara Brusky

want to attain motivation, then you have to let go of being discouraged. If you want to attain faith in the unseen, then you have to let go of doubt. If you want to start climbing your achievement ladder; you have to take that first step.

Today is dedicated to you. It's your day to celebrate the change in your life by changing the way you think, speak and act. This is your day to accept and be accountable for the way your life has been in the past. It's time for you to close the door to the past and open the next door to your future.

CHAPTER THREE

QUOTATIONS FROM BELIEVERS

On May 5, 2010, I was researching some web-sites for quotes that would confirm my beliefs about how we think, speak and act develops our reality. I stumbled across the jackpot of quotations on *http://www.quotationspage.com*.

I've included quotes that existed before Christ and many of them are from the 1800's. The profound answer that we are searching for in life has been in existence for hundreds of years. Each and every one of us was born with a pure mind and the unlimited potential to succeed in life. The hidden fortune within you was born when you came into this world. The greatest believers in the unseen have become the skillful achievers to fame and fortune.

I would like to share with you some of the quotes I found from the believers of the past. The first quotes are from a woman who was physically disabled, but she overcame her limitations by leaps and bounds. A true believer in the unseen was **Helen Keller (1880-1969). Helen was a US blind and deaf educator that became famous from her disabilities. Here are some quotes from Helen Keller:**

1. "No pessimist ever discovered the secret of the stars or sailed an unchartered land, or opened a new doorway for the human spirit."

2. "Self-pity is our worst enemy and if we yield to it, we can never do anything good in the world."
3. "The best and most beautiful things in the world cannot be seen or even touched. They must be felt within the heart."
4. "When one door of happiness closes, another opens; but often we look so long at the closed door that we do not see the one which has been opened for us."
5. "Many persons have a wrong idea of what constitutes true happiness. It is not attained through self-gratification but through fidelity to a worthy purpose."
6. "Never bend your head. Hold it high. Look the world straight in the eye."
7. "Optimism is the faith that leads to achievement. Nothing can be done without hope and confidence."

The following quotes are by Ralph Waldo Emerson (1803-1882). He was a US essayist and poet. Mr. Emerson has some of the most profound quotes, which coincide with everything I believe to be true in my book.

1. "All I have seen teaches me to trust the Creator for all I have not seen."
2. "All our progress is an unfolding, like a vegetable bud. You have first an instinct, then an opinion, then a knowledge as the plant has root, bud, and fruit. Trust the instinct to the end, though you can render no reason."
3. "Do not go where the path may lead, go instead where there is no path and leave a trail."
4. "Finish each day and be done with it. You have done what you could. Some blunders and absurdities no doubt crept in; forget them as soon as you can. Tomorrow is a new day; begin it well and serenely and with too high a spirit to be encumbered with your old nonsense."

5. "If I have lost confidence in myself, I have the universe against me."
6. "Make the most of yourself, for that is all there is of you."
7. "Nothing can bring you peace but yourself."
8. "Nothing great was ever achieved without enthusiasm."
9. "Those who cannot tell what they desire or expect, still sigh and struggle with indefinite thoughts and vast wishes."
10. "The reward of a thing well done is to have done it."

The following quotes are from Cicero (106 BC-43). Cicero was a Roman author, orator and politician.

1. "A happy life consists in tranquility of mind."
2. "As the old proverb says "Like readily consorts with like."
3. "The people's good is the highest law."
4. "The welfare of the people is the ultimate law."
5. "To be content with what one has is the greatest and truest of riches."
6. "Gratitude is not only the greatest of virtues, but the parent of all others."

The following quotes are from Samuel Johnson (1709-1784). Mr. Johnson was an English author, critic, and lexicographer.

1. "Few things are impossible to diligence and skill. Great works are performed not by strength, but perseverance."
2. "Hope is necessary in every condition."
3. "Self-confidence is the first requisite to great undertakings."

The following quotes are from Henry Ford (1863-1947). Mr. Ford was a US automobile industrialist.

1. "An idealist is a person who helps other people to be prosperous."
2. "You can't build a reputation on what you are going to do."
3. "If you think you can do a thing or think you can't do a thing, you're right."

On June 16, 2009, I found another web-site *http://www.inspirational-quotations.com* by Barbara Jean Olson. I'm not sure how I found this site, but I printed out the quotes from it and set them aside. I found the quotes a few days ago and they were tucked away in a folder, in my desk drawer. Now I know why I was meant to find these excerpts on the internet. These were meant for assisting me with my book right here and right now. The following inspirational quotes are from various authors, and they all have the spirit of believing in the unseen.

1. "If you really want to do something, you'll find a way. If you don't you'll find an excuse." *By Jim Rohn*
2. "Instead of fighting your problems, picture your way out of them." *By Vernon Howard*
3. "Assume that whatever situation you are facing at the moment is exactly the right situation you need to ultimately be successful. This situation has been sent to help you become better, to help you expand and grow." *By Brian Tracy*
4. "Your big opportunity may be right where you are standing right now." *By Napoleon Hill*
5. "All progress, all success, springs from thinking." *By Thomas Edison*
6. "The secret to productive goal setting is establishing clearly defined goals, writing them down and then

focusing on them several times a day with words and emotions as if we've already achieved them."
By Denis Waitley

7. "I never worked a day in my life. It was all fun!" ***By Thomas Edison***

8. "It is literally true that you can succeed best and quickest by helping others to succeed." ***By Napoleon Hill***

9. "Your incredible brain can take you from rags to riches, from loneliness to popularity, and from depression to happiness and joy—if you use it properly." ***By Brian Tracy***

10. "The winners in life think constantly in terms of "I can, I will, I am". Losers, on the other hand, concentrate their waking thoughts on what they should have done or on what they don't do." ***By Denis Waitley***

11. "Welcome the challenges. Look for the opportunities in every situation to learn and grow in wisdom." ***By Brian Tracy***

12. "Act the way you'd like to be and soon you'll be the way you act." ***By Dr. George Crane***

13. "Faith is daring the soul to go beyond what the eyes can see. ***By William Newton Clark***

14. "There are only two ways to live . . . one is as though nothing is a miracle . . . the other is as if everything is." ***By Albert Einstein***

15. "Open your hearts to the love God instills . . . God loves you tenderly. What He gives you is not to be kept under lock and key, but to be shared." ***By Mother Teresa***

16. "Faith is reacting positively to a negative situation." ***By Dr. Robert Schuller***

17. "I would rather err on the side of faith than on the side of doubt." ***By Dr. Robert Schuller***

18. "Where hope grows, miracles blossom." ***By Elna Rae***
19. "Without faith a man can do nothing; with it all things are possible." ***By Sir William Osler***

People have known for thousands of years how to attain the path to success, harmony, happiness and wealth. It seems the only way people find out about this hidden fortune is by searching for it on their own. You have been in search for the hidden fortune and you came across my book to assist you. Children should be learning about their hidden fortunes in grade school, high school and college. It would be a bonus for our children to know early on in life how to achieve their deepest desires. Can you imagine what your life would have been like if you were taught as a small child how to develop your skills to unlocking your hidden fortunes? How we positively think, speak and act would have been ingrained in our minds to always believe in the unseen. Our existence on earth would be completely changed forever. If we were taught to not fear the unknown, or doubt our intuition, or that we only know of the words "I can, I will and I am," we would all be in tune with our Creator and everything that prevails beyond what our eyes can see.

I've seen what fear, doubt and negative language can do to a person's life. When there's no existence of faith or hope; there is sadness, desperation and depression.

I would like to share a story with you about what happened to my life when I lost my faith in the unseen and I let fear, doubt and the negativity of other people influence my thoughts.

When my Stefan and I first purchased our tavern, I had all the faith in the world that this would be a very prosperous business. I was so confident that I took a mortgage out on our home to buy the business. I knew this business opportunity would be profitable for us. The first two years showed an incredible amount of growth and prosperity. In fact, money was effortlessly flowing into our pockets. We went on vacations, made double monthly payments on our mortgage, and stayed on top of all our bills. We were both positive and uplifting people!

Then in 2008, life drastically changed for us. Stefan and I split most of the shifts at the bar. My average shift was 17 to 18 hours, since I worked weekends and karaoke nights. It was usually 3:30 or 4:00 a.m., by the time I would get home from work. I had to be up by 5:00 a.m., so I could take my son Tom to the bus, and my other son Kevin had to wake up at 6:00 a.m. for school. Also, if I was at home after working a long shift at the bar, I had our youngest son to take care of and he was only two years old.

My whole attitude began to shift from being positive to negative. I continuously complained about everything at the bar. Instead of being grateful for having a prosperous business, I was whining all the time about the tavern and being exhausted. I was clearly on a road to destroying my life, and at the time I didn't even realize it.

My persistent negative thoughts took a toll on my health and my life. After being in contact daily with people who always complained about having no money, being sick or were just always depressed, I found myself to be just like them. It took about three months of intense negativity for me to get gravely ill. When I finally went to see my doctor, my blood pressure dropped to 70/50. I was diagnosed with pneumonia and the infection spread into my muscles. My physician wouldn't release me to go back to work for a month. I literally fell into the trap of a life that seemed hopeless and full of misery. God help me, I lost my faith!

It never occurred to me that being around negative energy from other people would affect my life in this manner. It took me a good six months after my illness to realize that all I ever thought and spoke about from the time I woke up, until I went to bed were people who complained about their lives.

The thoughts that consumed my mind were like demons. It's astonishing how much someone else's attitude and energy can influence another persons life.

One morning I had an inspirational awakening. I like to believe that this was a divine intervention in my life. I realized that I wasn't practicing what I preached. The so called "light" went on in my head, and I took full responsibility for my negative thoughts and language. I acknowledged that negative energy had taken control over me, and in the process I created a life filled with pain, chaos and financial disaster.

I prayed for God's guidance to set me back on the right path. It was shortly after this incident that writing this book became a persistent thought in my mind. I wanted a better life for me, my family and for the customers in our tavern.

It was through a negative situation in my life that the seed was planted in my mind for this book to be written. Now, my main objective is to help other people who are experiencing turmoil in their lives. You have to realize that for every road that leads into a problem, there is another road that will guide you to an answer. You start believing in your dreams, by wrapping your heart around your faith in the unseen.

CHAPTER FOUR

RECEIVING YOUR LIFE'S DREAMS

You now have arrived to the final stage of receiving your life's dreams. You've read about the stepping stones to achieving your dreams, and now it's time to make them become your reality. Every point in this book has been a process for you to stay on track with your dreams, and that will be a part of your life's journey. Every one of us has a magical source that exists deep within us. The question that I reflect upon the most in my mind is "why do people keep repeating the behavior that isn't benefiting them?" You have to understand that toxic behavior doesn't equal rewards. You have to change what's not working for you, by implementing positive thoughts and behavior. At some point in your life, you probably burned yourself from fire, or on something that was extremely hot. You quickly learned that burning your self caused pain, so now you're careful when you're around anything that's hot. This is just like your life; if you constantly have negative thoughts and negative actions, you will cause pain and discomfort in your life.

THE MEANING OF WEALTH

People typically associate wealth with an abundance of money or material possessions. In my opinion, the true meaning of wealth goes way beyond just having money.

Barbara Brusky

Wealth is a combination of life long bliss, companionship, friendships, ultimate health and money. If you think that wealth is just about money, let me ask you a few questions to ponder about in your mind. What good is money, if you don't have a loving partner to share it with? What good is money, if your health is deteriorating? What good is money, if you're lonely with no friends? What good is money, if you find yourself depressed, because you're lacking companionship, friendships, or ultimate health? What good is money, if you don't have your family to share memories with in your life?

Achieving your abundance of wealth consists of how your inner-self is willing to give these same fortunes back to the world out of pure love. If you hold greed, envy, jealousy, hate, prejudice or any other negative emotion, you will never be able to create your dreams into your reality.

You have to be true to yourself when you want to give from your heart. When I say "true to your heart," I'm referring to how you feel after you offered something to another person. If your intention for gifting your time or even an item doesn't provide you with a warm, generous sensation from within you, then there was no purpose served. When you give with a compassionate heart, there is no attachment, criticism, expectation or judgment passed onto the recipient.

In order to receive what you desire in your life, the process begins by transforming your inner-self. As you transform your inner-self, your transformation will exude to your outer-being in your words and actions. You will become what you've been searching for in your life. On your path to receiving your fortunes, you have to keep your focus on being grateful for all that you already have in your life. It seems that being grateful for what we already have in our lives would be simple commonsense, but gratitude has become just a concept that we take for granted. When the emotion of being grateful isn't felt from within, you directly turn off the flow of energy to all great things that can come your way. Being wealthy is such a versatile word, because many of us have already attained "wealth" in our lives, but we don't even realize it.

Part of your wealth is comprised of your family, whether that's having your own children, adopted children, a mother, father, in-laws, grandparents, aunts, uncles or brothers and sisters. I think back over the past two years, when my husband and I hit a financial crisis, and how our families bonded together to help us out. My gratitude goes above and beyond what words could ever express for my heartfelt appreciation. My in-laws financially assisted us, since we weren't able to keep up with our mortgage payments and all the other bills we incurred from our tavern and home. My husband has a wonderful job, but we haven't been able to make ends meet, since we couldn't sell our tavern.

There were times that our situation felt quite depressing, but I knew that these circumstances wouldn't last forever. At first, I thought our financial crisis was a punishment for something that we must have done in our lives. Now, I believe God had a purpose for us and as long as we were relying on the tavern to bring us money, neither one of us were living our lives to our fullest potential.

I realized that when we were making money at our tavern, my husband and I weren't using our talents. Stefan and I are now creating our dreams with our talents. I never would have been driven to writing this book if my circumstances in life wouldn't have led me to this juncture in my life. Also, my husband has been quite ambitious with his fly-reel business, which he designed and manufactured every reel part by hand. We are blessed in so many ways, and sometimes it takes our Creator to step in and change our lives to understand the path that was meant for us. Sometimes, we have to be knocked out of our comfort zone, before we realize what our true purpose is in life. For each time that my world has been jostled and I fell from the pedestal that I was perched on, I always gained wisdom, strength, and serenity after the passing of the storm. It's normal and healthy for us to express our emotions of grief and feel discomfort, pain and depression, when we are initially shocked by an undesirable predicament. It may be difficult at first to accept the problem, but we have to realize that we are exactly where we are supposed to be in life.

UNDERSTANDING MONEY WEALTH

The one thing that everyone seems to want is MONEY. Money tends to be the number one item that everyone wants and needs right now. The issue with money is that it controls what surrounds us. We need money in order to pay the mortgage, gas & electric, phone, cable/satellite, groceries, water, maintenance for vehicles and the list goes on and on.

Did you ever notice that what you are emotionally attached to is what you want more of in your life? When you're attached to something like money you fear losing it, envious of those who have it, desperate to get it and criticize those who effortlessly achieve it.

I'm not a stranger to these emotions, but I have figured out that you must learn to "let go" of the attachment to what you want. In order to let go of the attachment, you must have faith and let God take over your fears. Everybody has the power within themselves to summon what they want into their lives. You've been doing this for years, but you're using your creative powers and the Law of Nature against you. Let your intrinsic power work for you when you want something. Alexander Graham Bell believed in this hidden power and he stated, "What this power is, I cannot say. All I know is that it exists . . . and it becomes available only when you are in that state of mind in which you know exactly what you want . . . and are fully determined not to quit until you get it."

The majority of people in the world want to attract more money, so I will explain a few different methods about attaining your hidden fortune with cold hard cash.

RICH GET RICHER

There are so many people in the world who have money, and there is an explanation for it. People with money, think money and are determined deep within their inner core to keep money flowing to them. They are driven with a fire in their spirit and they see themselves receiving money before it even gets to them. Self made millionaires weren't sitting around and complaining about being poor, they were devising plans to make them money. Multi-billion dollar corporations didn't become successful with people who had low self-esteems and pessimistic attitudes. These corporations are founded on people who are high achievers, optimistic, and are completely engrossed with thinking, speaking and acting towards success. When you "understand what you want, you become what you want."

I'd like to share another story with you, which will help you understand what happens when you "let go" of attachment with money.

As a bartender, I've met a lot of people. One evening a gentleman from Lithuania came into our business while I was working. We had an extensive conversation regarding his life, because I was curious about his background, since he was a foreigner. Everyone called him Rif, because his birth name was too long to pronounce. Rif said eleven years ago he decided to come to America with only $300.00 in his pocket. He was in search of a better life for himself. He became a citizen of the United States, and enrolled at a Wisconsin University to pursue a degree in Computer Engineering. He worked full-time while going to college. After graduating with a Bachelor's degree, he went on to receive a Master's degree. Currently, he has an excellent job with a company in Milwaukee.

Rif never lost sight of his dream becoming his reality. He risked coming to another country and starting a new life, with a minimal amount of money in his pocket. There were times when he couldn't afford to purchase a small bag of sugar for less than $2.00, but that never discouraged him from giving up on his dream.

Rif has a burning fire within his spirit to conquer all barriers that may come in between him and his dream. He stayed focused on what he wanted to achieve and after he attained it, he was generous to the people around him. When ever Rif came into our tavern, he always left me a $70.00 tip. He didn't fear losing money; he welcomed it and shared the money with people he hardly knew.

GAMBLING WEALTH

Did you ever wonder why there are people who always seem to win when they gamble? Lady luck is always on their side every time they step foot into a casino or buy lottery tickets. I have some expertise or knowledge on this subject, so I'm going to share with you the hidden secret to winning at a casino. First, I want to make perfectly clear that this is not to be used as a quick "get rich" scheme. It's been only from my personal experience that I've been able to win when I've gone to the casino. I mentally applied my power to win money. I've been able to do this for as long as I can remember. I don't gamble for a living, but I like to gamble for the excitement and fun. My intention before going into a casino is to win. I knew I would win and so therefore I did win.

Most people who gamble, they want to win, but aren't determined to win. There is a big, big difference. You have to really feel the money coming into your life, as if you already won it. There is a thrilling stimulation that overwhelms your entire being, before you actually win the money. It's the unseen vision of money that I made become my reality.

In 2007, my husband and I won a substantial amount of money in hand pays from different casinos. If you are not familiar with the gambling term "hand pay," it means that when you hit a jackpot on a slot machine that is over $1199.00, an attendant from the casino will physically pay the money to you. We have every W-2 form, which we received from the casinos to prove our winnings and submitted them to our tax accountant.

The last time my husband and I vacationed in Las Vegas, I brought my gratitude journal with me. I wrote about how grateful I was to be on vacation with my husband, the beautiful mountains and sensational sunrises; that I saw from our penthouse room at Mandalay Bay. One morning in Vegas, I wrote about winning on a triple diamond slot machine. I specifically wrote that this triple diamond machine would pay out $7200.00. Well that same evening after dinner, I showed my husband the machine that would pay out this money. I had a terrible migraine, so I went up to our room to lie down. About an hour later, I went back down to the casino and walked over to the machine I was going to play, but my husband was already receiving a hand pay on it. He obtained three consecutive hand pays on that triple diamond machine and the money he won totaled $7200.00.

The deep secret to winning money is not to have an attachment to it. If you gamble with money that you know is for paying bills, you will lose that money, because you know that you can't afford to frivolously spend it. I have talked to people who gamble, and the ones that consistently lose usually walk away empty handed and with the thought in mind, "I never win when I gamble." People want to win money when they gamble, but they fear losing $20.00 in a slot machine. The fear of losing the money over powers the desire to win.

For me, I believe winning money is a bonus in life, but receiving money from your achievements is a victorious accomplishment to celebrate every single day.

ACHIEVEMENT WEALTH

Today I read an interesting article on my Yahoo home page. The article headline was "5 Secrets of Self-Made Millionaires" by Kristyn Kusek Lewis. I was immediately drawn to the story, because I wanted to know who these people were and what it took for them to achieve their goals in life.

There was one lady's story that I really was intrigued with, because she had a passionate dream that she believed in. Her name is Jill Blashack Strahan. Jill made $15,000 a year, and her husband could barely make ends meet with their bills. She had a dream about packaging and selling gourmet foods. Her husband passed away, which left her to raise her son as a single parent. Jill used the $6000.00 in her savings account, a bank loan and an investment from a friend, and started her business venture out of a shed in her backyard. Jill was three months behind in her mortgage payments, which led her to doubt her ability to achieve her goal. Her faith in the unseen dominated over her insecure feelings and she went on to building her fortune. Jill created the corporation "Tastefully Simple." She had $120 million in sales last year.

There is a tremendous amount of spiritual satisfaction when you can overcome the fear of losing what you already have in your life. If you tap into your highest power, which means believing that everything is possible in the world you live in, you will supersede any obstacles with your conviction to stay focused on your dream.

Jill made a statement in this article that sums up her positive attitude. She said, "I live by the law of abundance, meaning that even where there are challenges in life, I look for the win-win."

Thanks to Jill and her commitment to her dream, there are so many people who now enjoy her gourmet products, including me.

We are all born with the positive energy force, which enables us to strive to become whatever we "wish to be" in life.

MARRIAGE ~ RELATIONSHIP WEALTH

Wealth can also be defined with a successful marriage or relationship. A wealthy marriage is an extension of your love that is bonded to your partner's love. When you are personally fulfilled with your inner-self, it's easy to share your life with someone else. I can say from personal experience that a wonderful marriage makes the challenges in life easier to cope with. Also, when you have a wealthy marriage; you trust, inspire, support, accentuate your partners' qualities and believe in their dreams too.

There is something to say about having a meaningful marriage to someone. You feel as if you can climb any mountain, dream any dream, accomplish all your goals or even if you falter, your partner is there to stand you back on your feet.

Love in its purest form has no boundaries, limitations, expectations, or constrictions. Pure love is the foundation to all happiness. Whether your love is given to yourself, a marriage, a relationship, a friend, a family member or a stranger, there is only one form of it. When you share your love with another person, it should be given with no attachments. Love shouldn't cost the recipient any type of payment. Love is unconditional and free. It should bring joy, peace, laughter, and comfort to people. Love in NO way, shape or form contains pain, sorrow, fear, imprisonment, or hate. For me, I am anti "hate." I am so against the word that I've asked my children to replace the word with "dislike," when they use it in a sentence to describe something or someone. There's no room in this world that we live in to "hate" anything or anyone. Love can not flourish out of hate.

I am particularly astounded when people confuse their emotions with what they think is love. As an owner of a tavern, I've spoken to hundreds of people about their relationships. I'm not a psychologist or therapist, but owning a public business I've encountered a large quantity of people who mistake their emotions with love. It's been through my experiences as a bartender that I've truly discovered how lost people are when it comes down to "Love." I silently pray for customers when they pour their hearts out to me about their destructive relationships. I extend a part of my love to them in prayer and in friendship. I've explained to customers that love is not about controlling another person. If control and jealousy are involved in the relationship then you have no trust or true happiness.

Love should be the easiest, most sincere and most profound affection you can share with another person. "Love is patient; love is kind; love is not envious or boastful of arrogant or rude. It does not insist on its own way; it is not irritable or resentful; it does not rejoice in wrongdoing, but rejoices in the truth. It bears all things, believes all things, hopes all things, and endures all things." Bible, Paul, 1 Corinthians 13:4-7

Success derives from giving love, being loved and understanding love. You can start building your wealth of love every day by sharing it with the world that surrounds you. Don't let another day pass by you without extending your love with a smile, compassion, a hug, a kiss or a gentle touch of affection to another person. It's what you already have within your spiritual being that can be freely expressed each and every day. I promise you will feel an abundance of happiness as you generously share your love.

I'm going to close this chapter out with a story about how I came to realize the importance of love in my life and how it affected my spiritual well-being.

When I was 25 years old, I married my first husband. I thought it was the right thing to do, since my parents really liked him. We had two wonderful children together, during our ten years of marriage, but I wasn't living a very fulfilling life. After about seven years, I realized a part of me was slowly dying every day. I didn't feel as if my life had any personal growth or gratification. I became depressed and wondered if this was all I had to look forward to in my life. I loved being a stay at home mother to our children, but that wasn't enough for me to feel alive and passionate about my life.

My ex-husband's income was extremely good, but his money could not buy me happiness while we were married. I felt as if my life at home was a prison. After a couple years of feeling lifeless, a voice deep within me started silently screaming. I knew this was not the life that God had intended for me. When I was 35 years old, I filed for divorce. I sought therapy with a professional for a couple of years, and I learned how to be "me" again. I was a happier and more independent person. I felt as if I was given a second chance with my life to live as if every day had a purpose.

When I was 37 years old, I decided to date again. I used the Yahoo Personals web-site and thought maybe I would find a gentleman that I could share my abundance of love with. A year after being on the site, I decided to take my profile down. I spoke to God out loud one morning, and I surrendered my search for a partner to Him. I logged into my personal page to close the account, and there was one e-mail from a gentleman who requested if he could meet me. I wrote back to him and said "yes, I will meet you for a cup of coffee. A few days later, I met Stefan. He was incredible. We had so much in common. He didn't mind that I was divorced with two children and I was caring for my terminally ill grandfather in my home. My grandfather loved blues music, so Stefan would bring his steel guitar over to my home and play for him. I knew deep down that this was the gentleman that I would spend the rest of my life with. We've been married for 6 years and we have a son Waylon.

My spiritual well-being is so healthy and happy. I am fulfilled in every way possible. Every day my husband tells me, "I love you" and "you're so beautiful!" We have this bond that I can't explain in words. It's a connection of true love that I wish everyone in the world could experience. We are walking our divine path together. It is the best life a person can ask for and I have to give thanks to God for the gift of Stefan.

There is no amount of money that can be measured to the wealth of love. You are truly blessed if you have the love of family and friends around you.

MY CLOSING LETTER TO YOU

To my dearest readers,

Thank you once again for choosing to read "The Hidden Fortune within the Mind and Beyond." I pray that in some way I've shed a new perspective into your life on how to view that everything in life is possible. It's not easy to go through a difficult situation and always be able to see the lesson you can learn from it. That's why I stress that you have to keep your faith in the unseen. I'm not an expert in any professional field, but I have experienced many challenging circumstances in my life. My Creator has always guided me through the most violent of storms. There has never been a time where God abandoned me and left me without the strength, courage, or the love from my family and friends to overcome any obstacles that blocked my path to brighter horizons. I wholeheartedly believe that everything I've experienced in my life there's been a reason for it.

There is a purpose in this world for every one of us and we need to have an open mind and heart to live our lives to our fullest potential. We've been given so many gifts in our lives, and I realize it's easy to take them for granted. This is why it's important for you to keep your gratitude journal. When you tap into your heartfelt gratitude, you will find peace where there once was turmoil. You will find answers to your questions. You will find keys to unlock doors to opportunities. You will find an abundance of wealth in all areas of your life. We've been given this enormous universe filled with positive energy that we can harvest from to benefit our lives. I think the time has come for you to start using this positive energy to generate what you so desire in your life.

You absolutely deserve to live your best life. Every morning that you open your eyes greet the day with a smile and thank your Creator that you've been given another chance to make a difference in your world. You need to appreciate all that you can do and all that you can "BE." There are no restrictions for what you wish to become your reality. You're the only one who can put limitations on your dreams.

If you blame your current circumstances in life on things that happened in your past, it's important for you to "let go" of the past. The past can not be altered or revised. You can't go back and change it or wish it away. When I was a child, I experienced some horrible things, and it wasn't until I was in my 30's when I chose to seek professional therapy during my divorce, that I finally confronted my past demons and permanently closed that chapter of my life. When you carry your past baggage with you, you are cheating your self from achieving your most desirable dreams in life. Your past burdens only cripple you from thriving and prospering from accomplishing what you deserve in life.

If there are days where you find it hard to shift your thoughts, then re-read chapter 3. Remember that you can be just like these famous people who believed in the unseen. Don't give up on yourself, you have to take a leap with faith and strive to achieve your goals. You have to ignite the fire within your spirit and let it passionately burn towards your desires for success.

You're in charge of directing your life and the first steps to fulfillment are to be aware of your thoughts, words spoken and your actions towards other people. With positive persistent thoughts, words and actions, you'll be able to attain everything you wish to create in your life. According to the Dalai Lama, "If you develop a pure and sincere motivation, if you are motivated by a wish to help on the basis of kindness, compassion, and respect, then you can carry on any kind of work, in any field, and function more effectively."

You're the life support for your body, mind and soul, and it's completely your responsibility to nourish your positive thoughts to keep them alive. There's no one else who can believe in your dreams like you can. You are a special and unique person so cherish everything around you and count your blessings every day. Let your inner spirit brilliantly shine within you. You hold the power within your mind to create a better life for yourself so start celebrating your gift of life today.

If there comes a time where you're seeking a little motivational pick me up, you can find me on facebook. I look forward to sharing my inspirational thoughts with you. Here's an example of one of my facebook quotes that I've posted for my readers, "I am who I am because of my Creator. I only enhanced what he provided me with since I came into this world."

All my love and blessings to you,
Barbara